Mars on EAR...

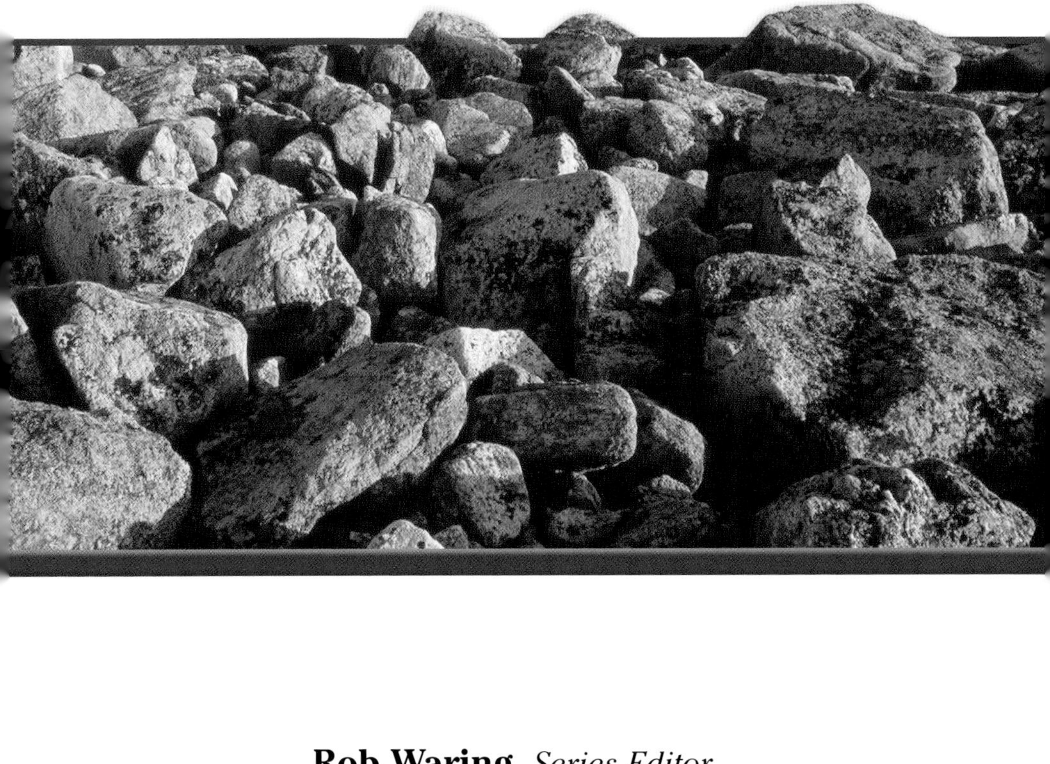

Rob Waring, *Series Editor*

HEINLE
CENGAGE Learning™

Australia • Brazil • Japan • Korea • Mexico • Singapore • Spain • United Kingdom • United States

Words to Know

This story is set on Devon Island, in the Arctic region of Canada. It takes place in and around a large depression in the earth called the Haughton Crater.

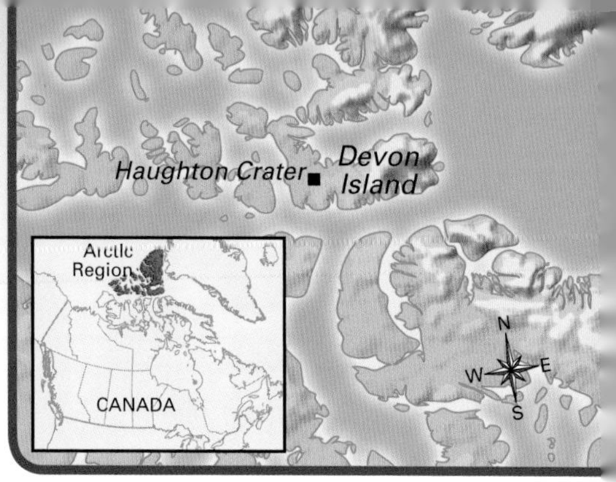

A Mars. Read the paragraph. Then write each underlined word next to the correct definition.

Scientists and astronauts have long been interested in traveling to the planet Mars, but its extreme distance and harsh atmosphere have created a number of challenges. The surface is freezing cold and the terrain is covered with deep craters so it's difficult to land on its rugged surface. Moreover, the atmosphere is filled with poisonous radiation and dust storms often occur. These barriers notwithstanding, NASA, or the National Aeronautics and Space Administration, anticipates having a person on Mars by 2037.

1. large holes in the ground: __________

2. sometimes harmful forms of heat, light, and energy: __________

3. the U.S. government agency in charge of space travel: __________

4. people who travel to and work in space: __________

5. difficult; hard: __________

6. the land or landscape of an area: __________

7. hilly; referring to land that is difficult to travel over: __________

B **Mars on Earth.** Read the paragraph. Then match each word or phrase with the correct definition.

Scientist Pascal Lee and his team have come to Devon Island to field test various equipment and device designs for future use on Mars. For example, they are trying out a 'thinking airplane,' and a space suit that will allow space travelers to endure the difficult conditions on Mars. They are also testing a special type of greenhouse that could help grow plants on the planet. This testing is especially important in helping scientists develop robust equipment and systems that can handle the extreme conditions on Mars.

1. field test _____	**a.** unlikely to need repair; tough
2. space suit _____	**b.** a uniform especially designed for space
3. greenhouse _____	**c.** test in a realistic situation or environment
4. robust _____	**d.** a building made of glass for growing plants

The NASA-Haughton Mars Project

On the remote and uninhabited island of Devon in the Canadian Arctic, day after day the characteristically freezing temperatures chill and the constant high winds blow across the **canyons**.[1] Despite the terrible weather conditions, which are to be expected this close to the North Pole, a group of explorers from NASA have set up a campsite in this harsh, unforgiving region. Tents and clotheslines full of drying towels dot the bare landscape. They belong to a group of people who are here for several months with the purpose of training and learning how to live and work on Mars, a planet that human beings have not yet been able to thoroughly explore. The group's members come from various backgrounds and nationalities, but they all share one common desire: to formulate support systems for travel to Mars.

Part of the explorers' work on Devon Island will be to field test equipment they hope will eventually be used on exploration trips to the distant planet. In effect, they are preparing for the day that human beings will be able to land on Mars. To do so, they've come to this alien landscape to experience life in an environment similar to that of the fourth planet from our Sun.

[1]**canyon:** a long, deep opening in the earth's surface

CD 3, Track 05

The planet Mars has a harsh terrain full of canyons, valleys, and craters.

Mars, sometimes known as the Red Planet, is an exceptionally harsh and **inhospitable**[2] place. The surface is freezing cold and the terrain is rough. At night, the surface temperature can drop to -73° Celsius*, and the atmosphere itself is poisonous for human beings to breathe. Add to those challenges the problems of radiation and dust storms and it becomes clear that surviving on Mars would be an impressive **feat**[3] of human intelligence and innovation.

Developing ways to overcome these challenges is what keeps researchers coming back to Devon Island each year. The rocky, treeless landscape of the island is actually a kind of 'Mars on Earth'; one that demonstrates conditions and terrains similar to those of the real planet.

---

[2]**inhospitable:** not welcoming; unfriendly
[3]**feat:** an impressive act, showing strength, courage, or unusual ability
*See page 32 for metric conversion chart.

Thirty-nine million years ago, Devon Island was hit by a large **meteorite**[4] that created a 20-kilometer-wide crater. Today, it's called the Haughton Crater and it almost exactly resembles the thousands of craters that cover the landscape of Mars. The similarity of terrain explains why training in the region makes perfect sense for scientists at NASA.

While it's safer and more realistically reached, Devon Island comes with its own set of dangers: unpredictable weather, high winds, and large **predators**,[5] such as polar bears, which may think human researchers could make a nice lunch! All of these conditions pose great threats, but despite the risks, project director and scientist Pascal Lee feels training here is what's best for the team's mission. In his opinion, training in a place that is very similar to the realities of Mars is an excellent opportunity. "By being faced with all the operational realities of having to explore a place for real," he says, "you are precisely building this experience to really plan an expedition where all these elements cannot be left to chance. You have to plan it well." That's why when Lee heard about Devon Island, he became convinced that it was the ideal place to train for Mars exploration.

---

[4]**meteorite:** a small body of matter from outer space that has landed on Earth

[5]**predator:** an animal that lives by killing and eating other animals

Infer Meaning

1. What does the phrase 'operational realities' on page 8 mean? Look at the words around it and write a definition.
2. What does the phrase 'left to chance' on page 8 mean? Look at the words around it and write a definition.

NASA

When some people think of Mars, they think of astronauts in space suits. Here on Devon Island, Lee and his team are, in fact, field testing the NASA Mars Concept Suit to see how it **withstands**[6] harsh conditions. Before it can be used in space, the prototype must undergo heavy testing and be subject to qualitative research. NASA needs firm empirical evidence that says the suit is safe in order to diminish concerns when using it in space.

The long testing process for the Mars equipment is not easy for the scientists and researchers involved. The suit is big, bulky, and, according to people who've tried it, uncomfortable and confining. Simply getting into and out of it is a slow and difficult process, but walking around with all that bulk often proves to be even more exhausting. In addition, the scientists must spend hours out on the open lands of the Haughton Crater examining and refining the design of the suit.

It's not always easy having such an unusual job, either. At times some of the scientists and engineers can be reluctant to talk about their work. Why? It seems that people often simply don't believe what they do. Stanley Kusmider, one of the suit engineers explains: "You're at the bar and you're talking to someone, and they ask you, 'Oh, what do you do?' [and I say] 'I work on space suits.' [And] they say,'Oh ho ho! That's funny! [You're a] funny guy!'"

---

[6]**withstand:** endure; bear

Depending on the perspective, designing a Mars space suit is either a great engineering challenge or a mechanical nightmare. Mars is incredibly dusty so the suit's outer surface will constantly be coated with a film of Mars' soil. This dust could erode most normal materials, so the materials used to create the suit must be resistant enough to withstand its effects. In addition, Mars is exceptionally far away, so astronauts will need to spend at least a year using the same suits day after day. For that reason, the suits need to be extremely strong, reliable, and easily repaired in order to survive for the entire duration of the trip.

Kusmider's colleague, another space suit engineer named Addy Overbeeke, has spent his career working on space suits, and he loves the challenge of making one for use on Mars. "You have to think about what they're really going to be operating in," he explains. "And [think] that 'Hey, this isn't it. We have to make the systems more robust and we have to make the systems more **user friendly**[7] for them to operate in [an environment] that's even more severe than this.'"

---

[7]**user friendly:** easy for people to use

The dust on Mars can be harmful to most materials.

Overcoming the severity of the atmospheric conditions on Mars is one complication astronauts face, but sustaining human life on Mars over a period of time is another issue altogether. It is a goal that raises a big question: can plants be grown in the harsh conditions of the Red Planet, thereby allowing food to be grown in order to sustain life?

Scientists believe that growing plants on Mars could be possible. Mars and Earth share many similarities. They both have about the same amount of dry land and have roughly a 24-hour day, which means that plants can conceivably be grown on the planet. The experimental growing of plants on Mars cannot be conducted at this point, so Canadian scientist Alain Berinstein is attempting to grow them in the Mars-like conditions of Devon Island. He's doing this by working on a computer-controlled, year-round greenhouse that simulates the scenario of growing plants on the Red Planet.

Berinstein explains how the greenhouse works: "Outside the greenhouse, you can see that there is a **hybrid**[8] wind and solar power generation system that charges a bank of batteries, and now we [have] our own independent power system in place. And so now we are running in a totally **autonomous**[9] mode with our own power and communications system that will allow us to operate twenty-four hours a day, twelve months a year." That means that the greenhouse can operate on self-generated electrical output even through the long, dark winter when nobody is living on Devon Island.

---

[8] **hybrid:** a combination of two types of things
[9] **autonomous:** independently operated

In addition to the space suit and the year-round greenhouse, NASA and the researchers are also field testing another new piece of equipment called the ‘Thinking Mars Airplane.’ Mars’s atmosphere may be thin and poisonous to humans, however it’s not too thin in which to fly. Therefore, researchers have proposed using a robotic plane as a substitute explorer. This UAV, or unmanned aerial vehicle, serves as an advanced **scout**,[10] designed to search for and photograph areas of interest. But a pilot doesn’t fly this plane, it thinks for itself.

Project contractor **Greg Pisinich**[11] calls the device ‘The Flying Graduate Student on Mars.’ In his opinion, it is similar to these professors assistants at educational Institutions. “You want something that has enough intelligence to make decisions, to look for the right science, to follow a hypothesis,” he explains. Just like a graduate student, who often does the preliminary work for more experienced educators, the plane likewise acts as an independent assistant to the explorers. On Mars, it would do the preliminary mapping work for the astronauts so they would know where they’re going when they reached an unknown area.

The images that the plane captures as it flies around Devon Island reveal an alien-looking landscape. And, while these test flights may seem like just fun, they’re actually serious research. The scientists are gaining insight as to how such a format could actually work once it’s used on Mars. It’s a step toward developing possible tools for future Mars explorers, and it’s also a great tool for those working on Devon. The NASA-Haughton team often needs mapping assistance in order to reach remote areas of the crater.

---

[10] **scout:** a person or mechanical device that collects information
[11] **Greg Pisinich:** [grɛg pɪsɪnitʃ]

Fact or Opinion?

Look at the following statements. Write 'F' for those that are factual, or 'O' for those that are an opinion.

1. The Mars space suit and the year-round greenhouse are not the only devices being tested on Devon Island. ______
2. The atmosphere on Mars is thin and poisonous to humans. ______
3. The 'Thinking Mars Airplane' is like a graduate student. ______
4. The flight tests are just for fun. ______

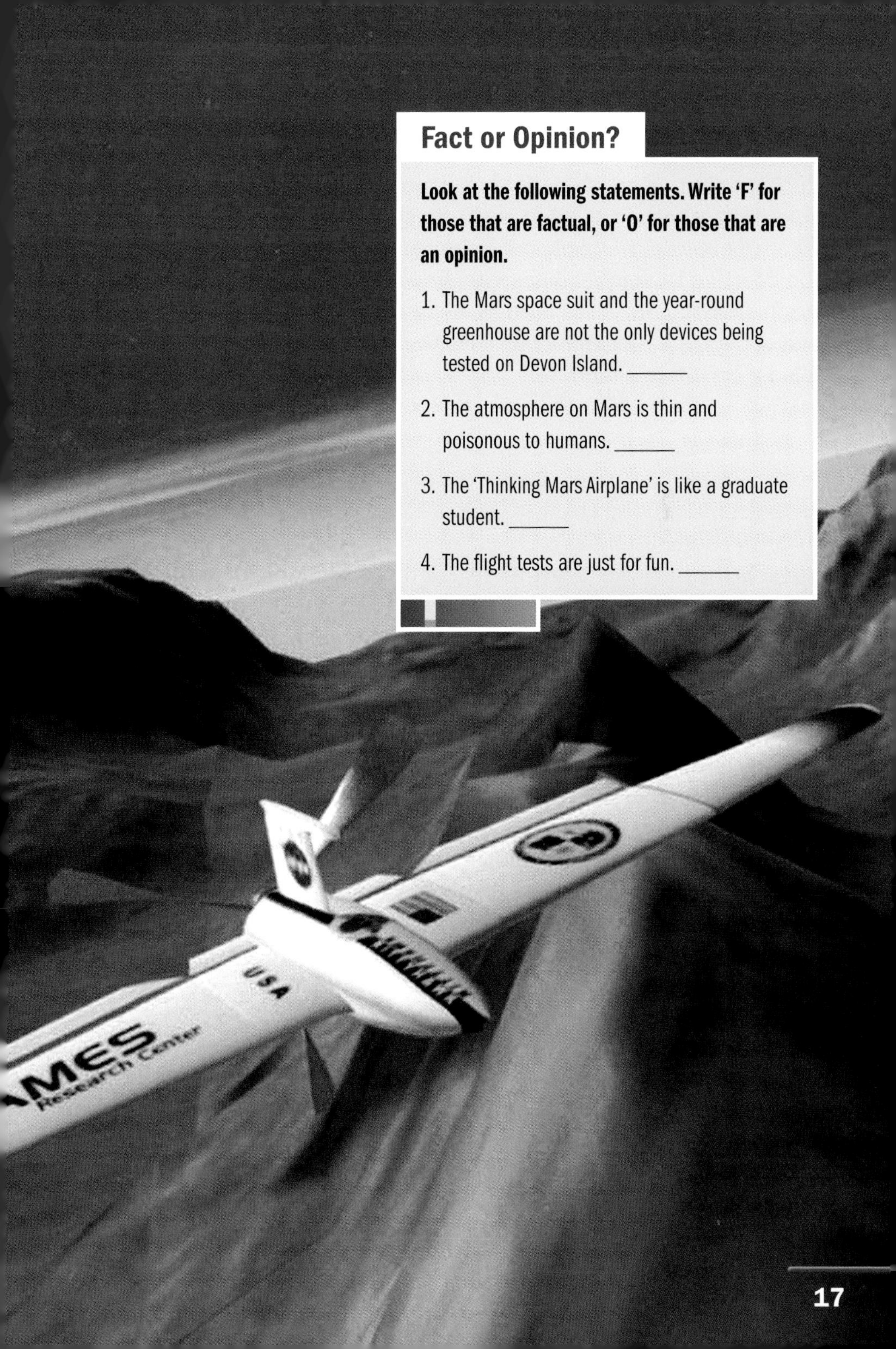

The next invention being tested on Devon Island is designed to be a reliable form of transportation used during exploration. If the Mars astronauts are going to spend six months traveling to the remote planet, they'll want to explore the place once they arrive. That's when the 'Martian Rover' becomes very important. The concept for the Martian Rover is a huge, heavy vehicle that can travel over the rugged terrain that Mars explorers would almost certainly encounter.

British scientist Charlie Cockell and expedition leader Pascal Lee are trying out the Martian Rover on an expedition to the coast of Devon Island. Cockell needs to collect some samples on the shore of the island and the Rover is the only way to get there. For this expedition, they are combining the technology of the Martian Rover with that of the Thinking Mars Airplane. Lee, who aims to be the first person to land on Mars, wants to push the limits of the Martian Rover. He wants to find out how far they can travel with the help of the aerial photos taken from the Thinking Airplane. He looks at the images taken by the plane, and plans the route of the Martian Rover accordingly. "So we'll head out from camp, go past the front of Marine Peak ...," he explains to Cockell examinging the transmissions from the airplane carefully. If they successfully reach their destination, they will have traveled further south than any previous Devon Island team.

the Martian Rover

a map of Devon Island

NASA's Bill Clancey has also joined the Rover expedition to the coast. He wants to learn how Lee and Cockell translate air photos into useful information to find the best route on the ground. Clancey explains what the information looks like, and is surprised at just how much Lee can understand from the images. "It looks like a piece of paper that has gotten wet and it's been **crumpled up**,[12] and it's just full of **wrinkles**,"[13] he comments. "And Pascal looks at this [paper] and sees valleys, these valley networks, and he sees canyons, and he understands cliffs and **gullies**[14] here. It's remarkable."

Lee, Clancy, and Cockell take off on their trip to the coast. As they travel, they seem to easily follow the route by using the photos sent from the airplane, which has traveled ahead. The result shows that the Martian Rover and the Thinking Mars Airplane are definitely compatible systems. It still takes time for the team to find where they want to go, however, mainly because the distances are great and the Rover moves slowly. As they creep along, Cockell jokes, "Are we there yet? I want ice cream!" A team member then jokingly replies, "Just ten more minutes!"

---

[12] **crumpled up:** pressed into a ball shape; lined and uneven
[13] **wrinkle:** a line or fold
[14] **gully:** a deep, narrow valley

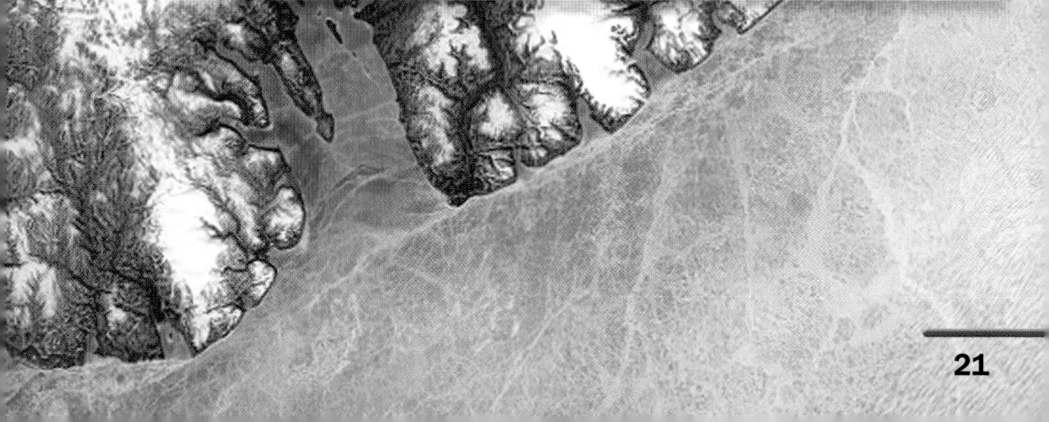

The three men carry on with their journey to pick up the samples on the southern end of the island. They're making good progress toward the coastline and the Rover is doing extremely well, rolling along steadily over the difficult terrain. They've now traveled further south than any other Devon Island team. Never has the island looked so much like Mars. There are red hills and valleys as far as the eye can see. The landscape is empty and deserted, but nonetheless it has a strange beauty.

The team continues to make great progress, but then Steve Braham, a fellow research scientist who's working back at the camp, suddenly calls them on the long range radio. A huge storm is moving in, he tells them, and the team is in its path. Storms on Devon Island can be dangerous, so Steve gives them an order: Come home now!

The worsening of the weather conditions requires the traveling to cease and the men have no choice but to cancel the expedition for the day. As Lee and the other team members start their return to camp, the sky blackens dramatically and the wind blows fiercely. It's disappointing, but even though they didn't make it to the coast, they know that their expedition was a success. They have managed to test key systems: air photos, long-range radios, advance scouting techniques, and the Martian Rover itself. They had anticipated some difficulties, but, they are well aware that in this harsh and remote location, simply returning to the starting point with everyone and everything safe makes the trip a success.

The field testing on Devon Island has proved to be valuable and effective, but when will the researchers be able to actually build systems for the harsh conditions on Mars? The whole team is impatient to do what no human has ever done: land on the planet Mars. It seems like a distant dream, but NASA anticipates putting a person there by 2037, a relatively short time considering the amount of work that the goal involves.

There is no way to know if a Mars landing will happen any time soon, but suit engineer Addy Overbeeke believes that it's only a matter of time, and preparing for that day is crucial. His philosophy is that human beings were meant to explore beyond their present limits. "We know that it's man's **destiny**[15] to go out and do space exploration," he declares. He then continues, "It's always time to think about what you want to do in the future." For these scientists, there's no better time than the present to begin preparing for their future, and they're doing it right here, their own version of 'Mars on Earth.'

[15] **destiny:** the influence of uncontrollable forces on the course of life and its events; fate

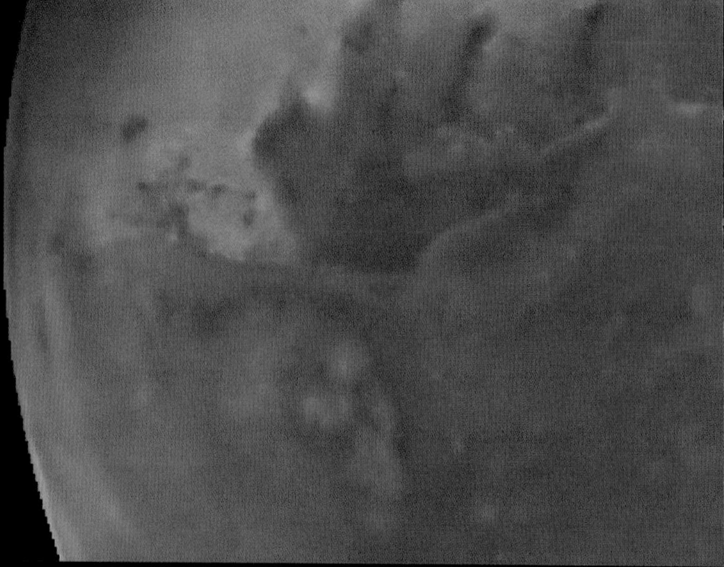

Summarize

Answer the questions. Then write a report about this story or tell a friend about it. Use information from your answers.

1. Why did the scientists come to Devon Island?
2. What devices did they field test?
3. Why was it important to test the equipment?

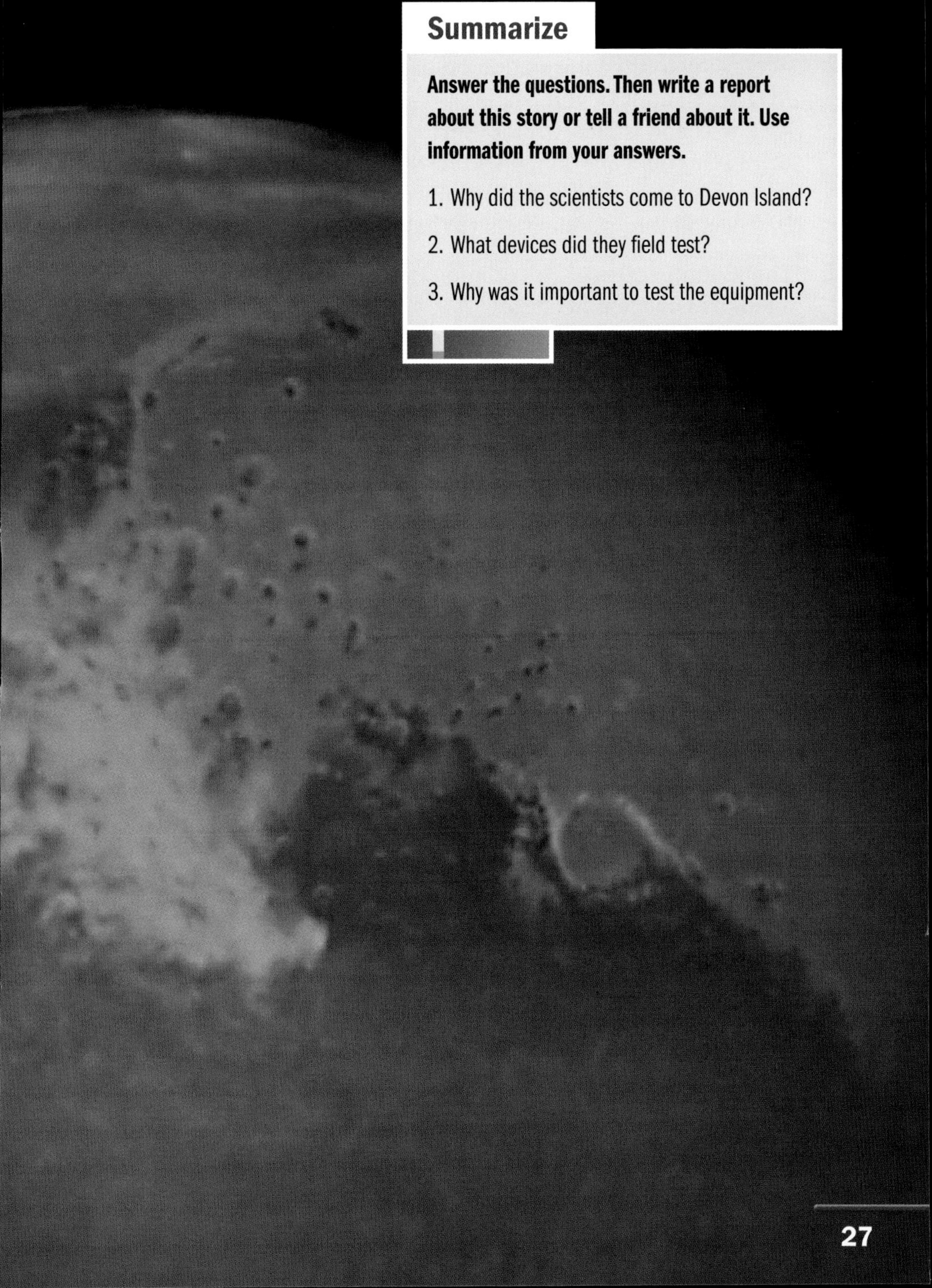

After You Read

1. According to the information on page 4, which of the following is NOT true about Devon Island?
A. The island is close to the North Pole.
B. Researchers are doing field tests there.
C. Temperatures there are usually extremely low.
D. The soil there is identical to that on Mars.

2. The writer expresses the opinion that surviving on Mars would be an impressive feat because:
A. Other explorers have failed before.
B. The conditions there are uninhabitable for humans.
C. NASA said it was impossible.
D. Scientists can't even survive on Devon Island.

3. What does the writer imply about polar bears on page 8?
A. They could be a danger to the researchers.
B. They like the same food as humans.
C. The explorers don't need to be concerned about them.
D. The explorers need special suits for protection from them.

4. Which word on page 11 is closest in meaning to 'observed'?
A. harsh
B. qualitative
C. firm
D. empirical

5. What does Addy Overbeeke mean when he says "Hey, this isn't it," on page 12?
A. The space suit isn't good enough yet.
B. The environment on Mars is too harsh.
C. It's impossible to be certain about the space suit.
D. His colleagues made a mistake.

6. Alain Berinstein's greenhouse operates __________ year round.
A. one
B. every
C. all
D. full

7. What is implied about graduate students on page 16?
A. They are able to fly airplanes.
B. They do a lot of preliminary preparation.
C. They might get to travel in space.
D. They are skilled at mapping.

8. What are Charlie Cockell and Pascal Lee using to guide their course in the Martian Rover?
A. photographs
B. only an airplane
C. plant and soil samples
D. maps from great polar explorers

9. What does Bill Clancey find impressive on page 21?
A. the airplane
B. the information
C. Pascal Lee's skills
D. the valleys, canyons, and cliffs

10. Why do Lee and Cockell end their expedition early?
A. They have an accident.
B. There is a miscommunication with Braham.
C. They have a disagreement with Clancey.
D. There is a change in weather conditions.

11. Which word on page 26 can be replaced by 'critical'?
A. valuable
B. effective
C. impatient
D. crucial

12. What does the writer most likely think about human exploration on Mars?
A. NASA won't be the first to send a team there.
B. Exploring Mars is going to be an impossible feat.
C. It may still be many years before it becomes a reality.
D. It's too far beyond the limits of human beings.

Space Times

FINDING A NEW HOME IN SPACE

The dramatic rate at which Earth's population is increasing each year, the rapidly growing pace of environmental destruction, and the radical climate changes due to global warming all signal trouble for our planet. Certain regions of the earth may someday disappear under water and others may no longer be able to provide enough food to feed everyone. For these reasons and others, scientists have begun to explore the possibility of creating places for humans to live and work other than on Earth.

The Moon

In 2006, NASA announced plans to create a permanent settlement on the moon by 2024. This community will consist of groups of scientists who will take turns living on the moon for a few weeks at a time. Their job will be to explore the moon's surface and conduct experiments to determine what must be done to create suitable living conditions so humans might later live on the moon full-time. One goal of the program is to find a way to create a moon community in which all the physical and psychological needs of humans can be met, and in which they can eventually operate businesses that will supply products to Earth.

Comparing the Possibilities

	On the Moon	On Mars	Space Stations
Travel Time	a few days	a few months	a few hours
Gravity	83.3% less than on Earth	62% less than on Earth	artificial gravity can be created
Water Supply	none	ice at the poles	must be created and recycled
Temperature	(lowest) -233˚C (highest) +123˚C	(lowest) -140˚C (highest) +20˚C	temperature can be controlled

An Artist's Impression of a Space Station

Mars

Plans for creating settlements on the planet Mars are not as well developed as those for the moon. At this point, most researchers are focusing on the possibility that Mars might be a good next step, primarily because of its similarities to Earth. Unlike the moon, Mars appears to have water, although most of it seems to be frozen under the polar areas. On Mars, days and nights are approximately the same length as they are on Earth. Although temperatures are considerably colder than those on Earth, Mars is still the planet most comparable to Earth in our solar system.

Space Stations

Many people believe that space stations may prove to be the best way to create permanent, non-Earth homes for large human populations. Research in this area is focusing on how to make the most of building a settlement that doesn't have the limitations of a moon- or Mars-based program. For example, Earth-like gravity can be created on a space station. The station can be located near Earth so that supplies can be moved back and forth quickly and inexpensively. Also, since a space station can receive sunlight 24 hours a day, such settlements would have a constant, plentiful supply of solar energy.

CD 3, Track 06

Word Count: 395
Time: _____

Vocabulary List

astronaut (2, 11, 12, 15, 16, 18)
autonomous (15)
canyon (4, 6, 21)
crater (2, 6, 8, 11, 16)
crumpled (21)
destiny (26)
feat (7)
field test (3, 4, 11, 16, 26, 27)
greenhouse (3, 15, 16, 17)
gully (21)
harsh (2, 4, 6, 7, 11, 15, 25, 26)
hybrid (15)
inhospitable (7)
meteorite (8)
predator (8)
NASA (2, 4, 8, 11, 16, 18, 21, 26)
radiation (2, 7)
robust (3, 12)
rugged (2, 18)
scout (16, 25)
space suit (3, 11, 12, 16, 17)
terrain (2, 7, 8, 18, 22)
user friendly (12)
withstand (11, 12, 26)
wrinkle (21)

Metric Conversion Chart

Area
1 hectare = 2.471 acres

Length
1 centimeter = .394 inches
1 meter = 1.094 yards
1 kilometer = .621 miles

Temperature
0° Celsius = 32° Fahrenheit

Volume
1 liter = 1.057 quarts

Weight
1 gram = .035 ounces
1 kilogram = 2.2 pounds